To the South Pole

written by
Annabel Ogilvie

illustrated by
Dennis Manton

Macdonald Educational

On January 14, 1911 Roald Amundsen and his party reached the Barrier—a huge wall of ice, towering 30 metres high, which stretched shining white across the Antarctic waters. To these men the Barrier was the gateway to their goal—that vast unexplored wasteland of ice and snow which drew them to the South Pole!

Their sturdy ship *Fram* had carried them 25,000 kilometres to bring them here. Now she sailed proudly into the Bay of Whales, a great inlet in the wall of ice, and landed on the Barrier.

Then began the long work of
unloading their ship and establishing a
base. Leaving ten men on board the
Fram, Amundsen and eight companions
trekked into the ice. By a sheltered ridge
of ice they established their home,
where the nine of them could live and
work, sheltered from the bitter cold.
They set their teams of dogs to work,
sledging to and from the ship they
brought up the many provisions that
had been so carefully assembled and
carried so far. The most painstaking
care had to be taken with these supplies.
Every detail had to be taken care of if
they were to survive in this bleak
wilderness, reach the far off Pole and
return alive.

By the beginning of February they had established their base. Franheim, as they called their home, was ready. Their 900 cases of provisions were stacked neatly in the snow and the dogs were happily settled around the hut.

Before the terrible Antarctic winter
set in the explorers had to establish
depots of supplies. When the spring
brought milder weather they could begin
their trek to the Pole and they would
have provisions distributed along their
route. Amundsen and three companions
put on thick reindeer skin clothing to
protect them from the bitter cold. With
three sledges loaded with supplies they
set course for the South Pole. Despite a
light fog they covered the unknown

ground fairly easily and in four days reached the spot where they set up their first depot. They marked the site and turned homewards. In two days of hard driving they reached Franheim. *Fram*, their last link with the outside world, had sailed to avoid being trapped in the closing ice. The nine explorers were alone on the Barrier. They now had to fend entirely for themselves in this snowy wilderness until their ship returned next year.

More depots had to be established and eight men set out for the second trip. With seven sledges and 42 dogs they carried a huge store of provisions. They were over-confident. The bitter cold and the heavy loads began to exhaust the dogs. They reached the first depot and pushed their way further southward, setting up a second depot and journeying onwards. Now they were travelling across ice where hummocks and cracks made the journey much harder for men and dogs. As they made their way across this dangerous land the three leading dogs disappeared. They had fallen into one of the deep crevasses that criss-crossed the route. Luckily the dogs were held by the harness attaching them to the sledge and were pulled safely to the surface.

The ice had given full warning of its
treacherous nature. Despite the terrible
conditions the party set up a third
depot but they could go no further. They
turned to make their way homeward.
At last they reached Franheim. They
had established two further depots but
in the process eight of their brave dogs
had died of cold and exhaustion. The
men too had suffered horribly. Now the
terrible Antarctic winter was about to
begin.

To make more space Amundsen and his men tunnelled through deep drifts of snow to make rooms in which they could work. The sledges were stripped to make them as light as possible. Alterations were made to clothing to keep the explorers safe from the perils of frostbite and snow-blindness. Their food and equipment was checked and re-checked and finally packed. Caring for the dogs and making their preparations kept the men busy throughout the long winter.

The men were impatient to be off and
on September 8 when spring seemed to
have arrived at last, Amundsen led his
men south. The dogs, having rested all
winter, were wild and unwilling to work.
The drivers eventually set them on the
route and the expedition was under way.
However, the Antarctic weather was
against them and the temperature,
which had been rising, dropped to the
freezing depths of many degrees below
zero. Amundsen decided to abandon the
journey and the party returned to
Franheim, frostbitten and temporarily
defeated.

On October 19 Amundsen started out
again. This time they would reach the
Pole or die in the attempt! He took with
him just four men and four sledges each
drawn by 14 dogs. This time the weather
stayed mild and they made excellent
progress, picking up supplies at each of
the three depots they had fought so
hard to establish.

After the third depot was passed they were on unknown ground. Guided only by their instruments they made their way across the Barrier, establishing further depots as they went. Losing only a few of their faithful dogs they soon reached the base of the icy mountains that blocked their path to the Pole. They soon knew that they must make their way up the great glacier which ran between the mountains. It was a very difficult route, but Amundsen and his men were determined to conquer it. The way might be hard, but it was the way to the Pole and they had to travel it.

The dogs worked hard on the steep ascent. Amundsen and his men pushed, pulled and coaxed them until at last they reached a place where they could camp. Here Amundsen and his men had to perform a terrible task. They could not take all their dogs with them to the Pole, only 18 were needed. So with sorrow in their hearts, the explorers slaughtered the animals. The dogs had done their best, but they must be killed and their flesh used to feed those that remained. The fresh meat was necessary to give extra food to the dogs, and the men too, during this last and hardest stage of the journey. They named this place 'The Butcher's Shop'. Mourning the loss of their faithful dogs, they rested there awhile. The rumble of nearby avalanches and the howling wind surrounded them.

They continued their journey in a blizzard which blinded them and froze their flesh as they struggled onwards. They came to another glacier, pitted with huge crevasses which could swallow dogs, sledges and men in their bottomless depths. Amundsen led his party across thin bridges of snow, skirting vast blocks of ice and climbing huge ridges that blocked their path. Thanks to their courage and skill they conquered the Devil's Glacier, as they named it.

A high ridge now blocked their path, but they made their way through Hell's Gate, a narrow gap, and on to the Devil's Ballroom. They were crossing this slippery surface when two leading dogs fell through the ice. They were pulled up by their harness and the hole examined. The party was crossing a paper thin layer of ice. A little way underneath was another layer of ice. Moving onwards Bjaaland suddenly fell. His feet had gone through the bottom crust of ice as well as the upper surface. He hung suspended by his arms over a bottomless chasm. Only his quick thinking had saved Bjaaland from certain death!

At last the ground levelled out and they had reached the polar plateau. Greatly encouraged Amundsen led the way forward. Suddenly he was stopped by a joyful shout from his companions who were all looking at their compasses. They had passed the point reached by the English explorer, Shackleton. They had now journeyed further south than anyone before them. It was a wonderful moment and as they unfurled the Norwegian flag Amundsen had tears in his eyes.

It now seemed certain that they would reach the Pole, but one fear haunted them. What if the British team led by Captain Scott had reached the Pole before them? What if their careful preparations, long journey and hardship had been in vain?

On December 14, 1911 when Amundsen and his companions checked their compasses they knew they had reached the Pole. They unfurled another Norwegian flag. They had won the race to the Pole by three weeks. It was a day that will go down in history. This bleak expanse of ice and snow was their goal.

By January 25, 1912 Amundsen had returned to Franheim. He had only 11 of his dogs left. He and his men were exhausted and their skins ravaged by frostbite. With great joy they greeted their companions at the base. The following day they relayed news of their victory to the crew of the *Fram* which had returned to collect the explorers.

Her decks draped with flags, the *Fram* sailed out of the Bay of Whales on January 30. Amundsen turned for one last look at the expanse of ice and snow which had been their home for more than a year. The Barrier was shrouded in fog and was hidden from the man who had conquered it and won his way to the South Pole.

Other Macdonald Adventures are:
Voyage of the Kon-Tiki
The Great Escaper
Battle of the Alamo
Pirate Treasure
Lawrence of Arabia

**Macdonald Adventures to be
published are:**
Curse of the Pharoahs
Ascent of Everest
The Search for Livingstone
Escape across the Mountains
The Wright Brothers
The Indian Princess